Bitterbrush

poems by

Phyllis Mannan

Finishing Line Press
Georgetown, Kentucky

Bitterbrush

*For David
and for Phil, Jon, and Elise*

Copyright © 2018 by Phyllis Mannan
ISBN 978-1-63534-492-9 First Edition
All rights reserved under International and Pan-American Copyright Conventions. No part of this book may be reproduced in any manner whatsoever without written permission from the publisher, except in the case of brief quotations embodied in critical articles and reviews.

ACKNOWLEDGMENTS

Thank you to the editors of these publications where the following poems or earlier versions first appeared:

Fireweed: "Redeeming the Thistle"
The Oregonian: "April Walk for David"
Rain Magazine: "Runaway," "I Have Stepped Outside of Myself"
Stringtown: "Otter Rock Mollusks"
Verseweavers: "Gatekeeper," Sections 1, 3, and 4
Willow Springs: "Three Dreams of the Everlasting"
Word & Image: A Dialog between Writers and Artists: "Runaway"

"Windpaper" was recorded by Oregon Poetic Voices and appears on their web site.

"April Walk for David" and "Runaway" appeared on broadsides for the Hoffman Center for the Arts Word & Image Project.

I wish to thank Oregon Literary Arts for a fellowship which helped to make completion of this book possible. Special thanks also to Nance Van Winckel, Christopher Howell, John Brehm, Diane Holland, Debra Brimacombe, Perri Gaittens, Stephen Sundin, Ron Bloodworth, and Mary Chase for their helpful suggestions.

Publisher: Leah Maines
Editor: Christen Kincaid
Cover Art: Elise Mannan
Author Photo: Elise Mannan
Cover Design: Elizabeth Maines McCleavy

Printed in the USA on acid-free paper.
Order online: www.finishinglinepress.com
also available on amazon.com

Author inquiries and mail orders:
Finishing Line Press
P. O. Box 1626
Georgetown, Kentucky 40324
U. S. A.

Table of Contents

Torn Fish 1

Glass Walls 2

Distressed 3

Redeeming the Thistle 4

The Wishful Undoing 5

Windpaper 6

April Walk for David 7

Flower Pot Song 8

Filling in the Days 9

Seeing Slant 10

Gatekeeper 11

Runaway 15

Three Dreams of the Everlasting 16

The Sluicing 17

Rubbed from the Records 18

Otter Rock Mollusks 19

Echolalia in Green 20

Blurred Portrait 22

I Have Stepped Outside of Myself 23

> *. . . all beauty depends upon disappearance,*
> *The bitten edges of things . . .*
> *   the uncertainty*
> *And dazzling impermanence of days we beg*
> *   our meanings from,*
> *And their frayed loveliness.*
>
> —Charles Wright, "Lonesome Pine Special"

Torn Fish

I can scarcely remember the first
time we came to this doctor,
David three, diagnosed *delayed*

as though he were a flight
that might land anytime. Now
twenty-five, he towers over

the other patients, unsnaps and
unsnaps one bright blue
or yellow Lego after another

until each boxcar in each
long train on the green carpet
has been uncoupled.

I sit with the weight of wanting
an unbroken story, watch
smug-faced fish circle

their glass house. A little boy,
peering, shouts, "Mommy, I found
a torn fish." She looks for her keys.

Later, alone in the waiting room,
I bend down, taking time
to examine reefs and seaweed.

Something white is wafted
by bubbles to the top
of the tank: a fish, splayed

at the spine, like two
fish, trying to swim apart,
thinly held by a tail.

Glass Walls

A fleet of doctors and students
came and went, peered unseen
through the one-way mirror.

Blond Dutch boy hair, red
corduroy, a tower of babble. What
could they say of our son—

a strange bird who pops
from the clock at 7:09 to trill
the wrong time?

Hadn't we fed him the right
sounds, bone-thin under
this blanket of glass?

At home he would have pulled me
to the cupboard, pushed
my arm at just the right slant.

Ort, toe. He means orange juice,
toast, I could have told them—
two on my list of ten codes.

Instead, his head-size was posted,
neck pricked in the one vein
that didn't hide.

Distressed

His teeth fluted
the edges
of the antiqued table,
wainscot cornice,
heirloom bed.

Two babies
in ten months
then a move.
Still his brother and sister
filled every room.

Behind the fence
a neighbor's
dog barked.
*Could it hurt
my face?* he thought—

and years later
said this to me
when he
could speak.
Now he was eight

and the sentence
splayed out
in little
even marks
along the wood.

Redeeming the Thistle

My mother climbed stone steps
in our garden, recapturing names
I might have called my children in a fairy tale:
Lithodora, Penstemon, Coreopsis Moonbeam.

She stared at my neighbors' front yard:
morning glory around roses, blackberries ripe
in the plum tree, quack grass bursting
through concrete, a few seeds
on bent dandelion stems. Worst
of all, the thistle.

"Grab a paper bag and get over there. Cover
those flowers before they go to seed.
Chop the bottom and cart
that thistle away!"

Later, I pulled my own crabgrass,
dandelions, a little oxalis. No thistles.
I remembered my neighbors worked long
hours, slept at their office, afraid
their microfilm company would fail.

I crossed the street to inspect the pariah:
tall … needle-spiked.
Brown flowers like bristles. Soft
purple down at the tip.

The Wishful Undoing

Columbia Gorge winds whistled over Portland.
Ice silvered the trees and built an igloo around us.

Across the kitchen skylight the Hinoki Cypress dragged
new claws. Our tabby groomed nervously.

"Walk on the barkdust, not the slippery,
falling-down ice," David warned himself

as he inched toward the empty mailbox.
On our hill, all services had ceased.

Two split-trunked maples plummeted
in our backyard—one, then the other.

A neighbor said the first went down just after
she looked at it; she wouldn't look out again.

We huddled by the hearth, David sticking
his elbow out like an awkward branch,

rolling his head side to side across
his chest—a slow pendulum of despair?

"We'll stop the wind, he said.
The trees won't fall down. They won't."

"The ones that already fell?" I asked.
"Yes," he said.

Two days later, looking into empty sky,
I heard two men unload chainsaws.

David ran to the window.
"They won't cut the trees. They won't!"

Windpaper

When the sheaf of unfinished poems lifted
from the small table and floated
to the ground next to our deck chairs,
David said "Windpaper."

In my memory, he'd spoken of wind
only twice before: first, when two
maples toppled in our yard and he pleaded,
"We'll make the wind stop."

The second time, walking home
from the beach, he said, "The wind stopped,"
as if he'd just noticed, after twenty-five years
of coming to the ocean, that trees
and houses block air flow.

I wish, now, he could tell me what kind
of wind lives inside the paper.
Will it take our uncertainties
and carry them
               across the sky?

April Walk for David

We walk the same circuitous paths
    his brother and sister ride
through bitterbrush and pine.

When his long legs take him too
    far ahead, I shout "Wait!"
Cyclists sing out from behind

"Passing on the right," and I pull him
    left. Once I got us
lost. Even blue and orange

arrows on the asphalt and a color-
    coded map could not
bring us home. *Yield … Yield.*

He pauses before the yellow sign
    at one intersection, runs
his fingers over the letters. "Stop?"

I think of Thomas, who had to touch
    Jesus' wounds …
those holes

in his hands and side,
    the only part of the Easter story
David understands.

Flower Pot Song

On the deck, flower pots float
on green saucers like lily pads.
The rain stops. David opens

the door, lifts the first geranium pot,
dumps water from its saucer,
ferries it across the sodden wood.

August, but it rains like November.
El Niño, the weatherman says.
"El Lean-yo?" David wonders aloud.

In the kitchen he sudses the brown
clay streaked with white fertilizer,
the way he washes his lunch box

after the bus brings him home,
the latches that won't
snap. *Rusted ... what is rusted?*

The way he scrubs white tennis shoes
going black. His nose drips: *clean
blood.* He takes out his handkerchief.

As he dries the last flower pot, he sings,
"Rain, rain, water down the drain,
wash and dry flower pots—"

words that tumble like socks
in a dryer, long after August.
As though a wagon keeps

appearing with one geranium. Before
he can plant it, the wagon rolls
back around the house.

Filling in the Days

A tall young man, his back to me,
inside the kitchen door.
Right arm raised, his pen twirls

a vapor trail one inch above
the wallpaper's notched leaves
in the margins of August.

His hand shakes, a lithium tremor,
as he writes, adding more tendrils
to the air above the leaves.

On his left, inside a white frame,
I see my own black notations: *Hair
appointment, Coffee with Perri.*

If I asked, "What are you doing?"
he'd say, "Filling in the days,"
and interrupted, put his pen away.

Outside the door I watch him stop,
look. His lattice sways. He parts
the leaves and slips through.

Seeing Slant

David pauses
by my chair,
lightly touching
the brick-red book of poems
called *Rose*
I hold in my lap.

On its cover
a chalked eye
with white lashes
drips like a tear
from a white cane,
a symbol of the poet's
father's blindness.

After our son's birth
the doctors said, He has
a small white spot
on his right eye. It won't
cause a speck
of trouble—not
a pebble in his field.

It's true he can see
a sudden rain dot
white rocks on the beach,
turning them
to Dalmatians,
then black Labs,

but he points
to the red cover,
its cane
with the glittering eye,
and asks, "Is that book
about the Good Shepherd
at Christmas-time?"

Gatekeeper

1

A gull stands, affixed to its image
on wet sand, one pair
of pencil legs wed to the other.

While we were gone, high winter tides
chewed the grassy dunes, leaving
a frizzled beard of roots,

huge logs, splinters spewed
all the way to Ocean Road, a six-foot drop
to walk along the surf.

As I stride toward the mountain, fog
takes me in. Basalt softens,
becomes mind.

2

David sits on a deck chair
in the cool morning sun,
vapor rising from his wet hair
as fog lifts from the mountain.

When he was ten, he tore the edges off
only the photographs he loved
most, then slipped them back
behind their transparent wall:

Goofy on Electric Avenue, hat and jacket
tattered by his tearing. Mickey,
ears notched, white glove
missing a thumb, waving.

Did he wish to make of them
one big picture in which all things
fit? Or was he simply helping them
to disappear?

3

Seek higher ground, the sign
warns … don't return
after the first big wave. Dotted

lines show the evacuation route.
Stark words explain the Monday
drills. I feel the sinking—all

breath gone, like a swimmer
who's swum too far out, flailing
under the legless sea.

A rosy light over the sky,
I think, *Yes,*
I must have died.

A wall of water thunders
through the mountain's sea
cave, closing my eyes.

4

Tremors rock my night-clad
body, drifting
in its blue lagoon, an arm
looped around me.

Cradled in the long chute
of waking, I hear
my husband's breathing
next to me

and the waves' soft
murmur beyond
our house, their white
lips opening and closing.

I drift out of dream
and breathe with the sea.

5

The house breached … footprints
in wet sand the only sign.

Three a.m., a scrape, a slam—a shadow
flying to David's window
to be let in, to have itself
stitched back like Peter Pan's
hours after it slipped away.

David hears a tap, throws
the net out. *If only my brother
would sleep in a drawer.*
A shadow spinning loose
must be tied down.

Disney books line David's
shelves. Above his bed,
an Indian woman, wooden
on a donkey, gazes down

at a swaddled infant
laced to a board.

In the next bedroom,
graffitied rock posters,
a gunspray of socks
and torn t-shirts, a whiff
of pot. Sheets like puffed up
clouds, no boy in them.

In the morning, David rubs
his fingers inside the white bowl
in the kitchen cupboard. *Where
are my quarters for hot
chocolate, my bus pass?*

Days later, two policemen drag
his brother down the blue
stairs by his long red hair.
"They won't pull
Jon's hair, they won't."

For months he opens
his window late at night, sets
an extra place at the table
for supper, strictly
aligning the fork and knife
beside the round white plate.

Runaway

It's like chasing
  a shadow,
    the officer said,
      refusing
    to track a teenager
who wanted to run.

Taking up the hunt,
  I traced
    a serpentine
      through the city
    where shadows
are sons,

the silhouette
  slipping in
    and out of other
      shadows,
    blending into
other shade,

but sometimes
  lying still,
    waiting
      for something
    to move
so it could follow.

Three Dreams of the Everlasting

1

Mud piled on my house. Mired.
I shovel it like snow until the ground
becomes a mountain range with me caught
in its center. It's not the darkness
I mind, but the weight and mass,
the sheer formlessness, of mud.

2

In a gully I look long
at a tall bank of packed earth.
I want to slice it like bread
to make sandwiches for my children,
but it is fouled—top to bottom—
with unwound spools of grass.

3

In the cool underbelly
of my house, a dirt cellar
where thick girders span the floors,
I look, not for turnips, or even
dirt-clumped potatoes,
but pale, oval, Bartlett pears.

The Sluicing

On an inclined trough, I dream away
impurities. A gate at the head

regulates flow. Even in sleep, I hear
the gate creak open, grind

shut. Over the log of my body,
the sluice releases water, lifting dross.

By morning, only silt—fine
sand—will be left in the flume.

Rubbed from the Records

The finger printer rolls each digit,
    black ink pad to white card block,
nail edge to nail edge.

It rocks in her hand and signs
    its name: loop, whorl, delta, arch,
leaf, petal, spiral shell—

but imperfect. A smudge marks
    the mouth of two rivers.
Low papillary ridges, dry plains.

She looks for clarity
    my fingers do not know,
their skin smooth as erasers.

My prints come pack twice
    rejected by the FBI, the Teacher
Standards and Practices Commission.

Still I go on teaching, breathing,
    as if in some extremity
I might be found.

Otter Rock Mollusks

Our school bus swings away
from tide pools of eelgrass,
spiny-skinned urchins, lined
chitons. Students are slamming down
windows, sticking to green
plastic seats. Pale chaperones,
we settle into our own oceanic stew.

Wafted by currents we do not
understand, ninth graders rake
each other's hair, ink each other's
skin, and shuttle crunchy morsels
toward each other's lips,
where someone's jaw traps them
in bony plates. One boy,
hatted and headphoned, pulls
a jacket to his chin and digs
a sheltering hole, as a girl with purple
hair and navel ring beats
a tattoo on his head.

Tired after getting up at 3:30 a.m.
to catch a low tide, bathed
in fumes from the school bus
ahead, and melded to engine drone,
we bump north on 101—limpets
in a beautiful, boxy, bright yellow
shell, attached to the same rock.

Echolalia in Green

> *Thirty-two incidents of verbal disruption and wandering.*
> *Crossed Alexander Street to throw paper over a fence.*
> *Nearly hit by a car.*
>   —Incident report, Tualatin Valley Workshop

On our front door, a bare grapevine wreath
from the basement. No flowers, no ribbons,
just brown woody stems thrust in a circle, stubs
poking out—last year's Lenten crown of thorns.

"Where's the Cub Scout wreath?" I ask David
as I drop shopping bags by the door. The fragrant green
one with the prim red bow. Face dark, he intones,
"Monday, Tuesday, Wednesday, go work, go home."

~~~

"Your son drives me nuts; he talks all the time,"
a young woman says when I visit his workshop—
a huge pile of screws on the table,
workers counting them into small plastic bags.

At home, I hear David's voice boom,
"Close the mouths up or I'll break your arm!—"
an echo of someone fed up with his talking.
All those mouths keep giving him trouble.

"Whatever being quiet is," he mutters,
spewing other people's messages like a skewed
answering machine, his arms swinging wildly
as he powerwalks the house.

Christmas Day he's caught in a chant,
repeating a path through relatives' rooms.
"I'll be quiet," he shouts. "I won't be up,
down, back and forth anymore!"

~~~

In January we buy a green van, start seeing
Dr. Ed Green—Dr. Greenstubs, David calls him
(his last psychiatrist was Gene Stubbs). His office
is a house with green shutters, green awnings.

"Will you come back and see me on St. Patrick's Day?"
the new doctor says. "Be sure to wear green."
In February I find the Cub Scout wreath
on the far side of our fence. David plucks off its red bow.

Blurred Portrait

I pulled the trigger. Blue window cleaner
shot foam over the smudged glass and frame.

Gray-green eyes, white points at the center
of each iris, tongue pressed

shyly to his lower teeth, smiling,
silky yellow hair—an eight-year-old gone

under spray. As in the bathroom now, twenty years
later, David smooths too much shaving cream

over his cheeks, down his neck, hands me
the razor. "Will you help him … help her?—"

his pronouns blur. My hand pulls
the plow down, parts the snow.

I have Stepped Outside of Myself
    —*The Wiz*

I'd pull a costume over my head and slink
across a stage. Pull the cape to my neck.

Let green shades sprout from ears,
delicious schemes roil under a hat.

But the lovelorn costume maker won't
re-sew a stitch—won't restore

the scarecrow torn in capture
or replace the pin in the tin man's heart.

Windows crash, broken roof shingles
shatter through the scrim.

The wizard must toss away his suit. Pieces
of his city fly out on either side of the set.

"You've got to peel off all your clothes,"
he says, "to find out who you are."

I think he's wrong—my self
a sack of straw holding a crown.

Phyllis Mannan began writing about her son David, who has autism, in an attempt to understand him and to discover what happens to relationships when the ability to communicate and understand feelings is severely limited. Through her poems and nonfiction stories, she hopes to give her son—and perhaps others with unique ways of thinking—a voice in the world.

Phyllis has received an Oregon Literary Arts Fellowship in Poetry, and her poems have appeared in *Cloudbank, Fireweed, The Oregonian, Rain Magazine, StringTown, Verseweavers, Willow Springs,* and other publications. Her nonfiction story, "Pot Roast Coming Around the Clock," appeared in *A Cup of Comfort for Parents of Children with Autism.* Her memoir, *Torn Fish: A Mother, Her Autistic Son, and Their Shared Humanity,* published in 2015, asks, "What happens when a child with autism grows up?" and "What makes us human?"

As an advocate for adults with developmental disabilities and their families, Phyllis has served on the Board of Directors of Edwards Center and Bethesda Lutheran Communities Family Association. A former high school English teacher, she lives with her husband on the north Oregon coast.

www.ingramcontent.com/pod-product-compliance
Lightning Source LLC
LaVergne TN
LVHW050046090426
835510LV00043B/3330